TWEEN TALK

A TWEEN'S GUIDE TO SOCIAL SUCCESS

ERAINNA WINNETT, Ed.S.

Tween Talk: A Tween's Guide to SOCIAL SUCCESS
Text © 2014 Erainna Winnett
Cover Design Chamillah Designs
Interior Layout Streetlight Graphics

Library of Congress: Cataloging-in-Publication Data
Winnett, Erainna
Tween Talk: A Tween's Guide to SOCIAL SUCCESS
Summary: Discusses issues facing children aged 9-12 such as dealing with bullies, cyberbullying, peer pressure, and conflict resolution. Also included are ways to handle cliques, foster friendships, and ignite confidence.
1. Bullying—Juvenile literature. 2. Cyberbullying—Juvenile literature. 3. Social Skills (Friendship, Peer Pressure, Conflict Resolution) (Psychology—Juvenile literature).

ISBN: 978: 0692211182
ISBN: 0692211187

CounselingwithHEART.com

Printed in the United States of America
10 9 8 7 6 5 4 3 2 1

DEDICATION

To Jeana,

my tween best friend in 1980

"Great people do things before they're ready. They do things before they know they can do it. And by doing it, they're proven right – because I think there's something inside of you and inside all of us, when we see something, and we think, 'I think I can do that. I think I can do it. But I'm afraid to.' Bridging that gap, doing what you're afraid of, getting out of your comfort zones, taking risks like that...that is what LIFE is."

– Amy Poehler

THIS BOOK BELONGS TO:

_____

A tween whose journey to success begins TODAY!

TWEEN TALK

A TWEEN'S GUIDE TO SOCIAL SUCCESS

WHY SHOULD YOU READ THIS BOOK?
BECAUSE IT WILL HELP YOU ...

- **Ignite Confidence!** Understand what builds confidence and what breaks it down.

- **Embrace Peer Pressure!** Tell the difference between negative and positive peer pressure so you can overcome the negative and embrace the positive.

- **Foster Friendships!** Create friendships and know the difference between cliques and *real* friends.

- **Become Bully-Proof!** Not BULLET-proof (which would also be really cool), but BULLY-proof. Learn what bullies look for and what cyberbullying is about ... especially with cell phones and social networking.

- **Promote Kindness!** Not only to *others*, but also to *yourself*, both of which will help you be successful.

I think every kid your age is pretty awesome, but following the advice in this book will help you make your life *even better*, maybe even SUPER awesome.

GETTING THE MOST FROM THIS BOOK

THREE IMPORTANT TIPS FOR READING THIS BOOK:

✓ **Tip #1:** Read a chapter a day at whatever time of day is best for you to read. Don't stay up past your bedtime to read it—I don't want teachers across America blaming ME for YOU being a zombie in class! Seriously, though, a chapter a day gives you some time to think about what you've read rather than just rushing through it all and then not remembering the important stuff! Taking it slow will help it stick in your head.

✓ **Tip #2:** If you read a whole chapter in less than 30 minutes, you're reading too fast. Slow down! There was a pop song back in the 1990s that had this to say: *You get to know things better when they go by slow.* It's true! Take your time with it—which means reading a chapter when you have the time to put into it, as in NOT 15 minutes before your favorite TV show comes on, right? I think you get the picture.

✓ **Tip #3:** When you're finished reading the book, put it in a special place on your bookshelf.

Mark a calendar six months from now. Why? Because you're going to read the book AGAIN. What? Am I crazy? Maybe, but that's beside the point. What I do know is that all kinds of things happen during your tween years from ages 9 to 12, and you'll definitely want to be reminded of everything in this book as you go along. Some of the stuff you don't need at one age suddenly turns out to be really important at a different age. An added bonus is that when you reread the book, you'll automatically think about how things have gone for you since the last time you read it, and that's always a good thing to do!

TABLE OF CONTENTS

INTRODUCTION

WHY I WROTE THIS BOOK FOR YOU

I WROTE THIS BOOK FOR you. I didn't write it for just anyone. I specifically wrote it for YOU.

You may be thinking, "Uh, how is that possible since you've never even met me?" Okay, you've got me there. I haven't met YOU, specifically, but I've met LOTS of kids like you—not **exactly** like you, because everyone is different—but **kind** of like you. I've worked with children for the past twenty years as a classroom teacher and school counselor. I've even raised two of my own kids. That's a LOT of years being around kids your age—the *tweens*, as you're called. I've watched you tweens very carefully over these years, and I think I've learned quite a few things that can help you.

IT'S NOT THAT EASY BEING A TWEEN

I'VE SEEN FIRSTHAND JUST HOW hard being a tween really is. You're not a little kid anymore, but you're not all grown up, either. You're, well, in-beTWEEN, so to speak. And that's a tough place to be. For many of you, your body is changing so fast, you can barely keep up with it. Some of you are well into puberty, while others of you are still wondering when it's going to start. And that puts your emotions all over the place as well. One minute you're happy, and the next minute you're sad or super frustrated. You don't know how to handle these powerful feelings when they happen, which makes you look immature to other people. It can feel as though you're on a roller coaster, as in exciting but also scary and maybe even a little nauseating ...

Then you have all the crazy stuff that happens at school—trying to be a good student in the midst of what sometimes feels like complete chaos. You've got some kids trying hard, others acting out all the time and disrupting the class, and maybe even a few who clearly don't want to be there at all. The chaos can make it hard for you to concentrate!

HOW THIS BOOK CAN HELP YOU

THIS BOOK IS DESIGNED TO help you make a smoother transition from preteen to teen by focusing on a bunch of things you'll probably have to deal with during these tween years. I'm going to share with you the best information I have about the following topics:

- Bullying

- Cyberbullying

- Peer Pressure

- Cliques

- Conflict Resolution

- Friendships

- Empowerment

If you're not sure what some of those things are, just hang in there—you're going to find out. So let's get started!

CHAPTER 1: BEHIND BULLYING BEHAVIORS

WHAT IS BULLYING AND
HOW CAN I STOP IT?

THERE'S A LOT OF TALK in school these days about bullying. In fact, sometimes you may feel as though it's all you ever hear about! The thing is, it really is a big problem everywhere. Ask yourself these questions:

1. Has anyone ever picked on you?

2. Have *you* ever picked on anyone?

3. Have you ever been threatened?

4. Have *you* ever threatened anyone?

I'll bet you can probably answer yes to questions 1 and 3, and you might even be able to answer yes to questions 2 and 4. Either way, if you can answer yes to *any* of these questions, think about how many other kids can probably answer yes to them as well. Can you see how bullying is a big problem everywhere?

Picking on kids or threatening them is a bad idea, for lots of reasons. The simplest reason is that it's *wrong*! In this chapter, I'm going to show you what to do about it. If you help put a stop to bullying, that's kind of like being a superhero, right? Just don't start coming to school in a superhero costume ... that would be a little weird.

WHAT EXACTLY IS BULLYING, ANYWAY?

 SOMETIMES YOU MIGHT NOT BE sure what bullying really is, so I want to help you get it straight in your mind. Kids your age tease each other, and that can be a little annoying, but as long as it's just occasional joking around, it doesn't qualify as bullying. But if it gets to be more serious and happens a lot, it

might start to become bullying. One way to define bullying is this: *actions that are unwanted and aggressive that are repeated.*

If you are being bullied, or if you are doing the bullying, the bully is using his or her power—such as physical strength, or knowledge of something embarrassing about the other person, or even his or her own popularity—to hurt or control others, and the bully keeps doing it again and again. The problem with bullying is that it doesn't just hurt the person right when it happens. It can actually affect people for the rest of their lives. That's not very nice, is it?

THE TRIPLE WHAMMY OF BULLYING

Whammy
Whammy
Whammy

THERE ARE *THREE* DIFFERENT TYPES of bullying that I want you to know about. The first is *verbal bullying*. This is when a bully uses words to hurt people. The second is *social bullying*, which is when the bully hurts someone's reputation or relationships with other people. The third is *physical bullying*, which is when the bully hurts people by punching, kicking, hitting, biting, or any other kind of physical attack. It can also involve destroying someone's things. Now let's take a closer look at each type of bullying.

17

Verbal bullying involves mean things being said or written about someone, which can include teasing, calling the person names, taunting, or verbally threatening to hurt him or her in some way. Ask yourself these questions:

Have you ever been hurt by something someone said or wrote about you?

Have you ever said or written something mean or hurtful to someone else?

You've probably heard the old saying: *Sticks and stones can break my bones, but words can never hurt me.* Well, I'm here to tell you that is NOT TRUE. Words can and do hurt people. In fact, saying nasty things about someone can hurt him or her much more deeply than hitting the person with a stick or a stone. When someone gets hit, that pain goes away pretty quickly. But the mean words that are said live on in that person's head, hurting him or her over and over every time he or she thinks about it. It can take a really long time for that kind of hurt to heal. And sometimes it never goes away at all.

I remember when I was a tween that a kid in my sixth-grade class didn't have clothes as nice as everyone else's. I think he may have come from a family that couldn't spend much money on buying him clothes that were in the latest fashions. His clothes were probably used or handed down from older brothers. There was this one girl who would make fun of him almost every day, saying something mean like, "Hey, where did you get that outfit—from the Salvation Army?" Can you imagine how he must have felt, hearing mean things like that almost every day? If it had happened only once, it wouldn't have been bullying, but because it happened all the time, it really was bullying, and the boy was clearly upset that he didn't have cool clothes like everyone else.

Social bullying, also called *relational bullying*, happens when someone's relationships with others or their reputation is hurt. This includes purposely leaving someone out, spreading gossip about someone, telling others to stop being friends with someone, or embarrassing someone on purpose. This kind of bullying can happen without you even knowing about it, at least until you find out it has taken place. Ask yourself these questions:

Have you ever been left out of a group of your friends? How did it make you feel?

Has someone ever said or done something that caused you to be embarrassed in public? How did that make you feel?

 One time when I was helping out backstage during a performance of the *Nutcracker*, I noticed a group of girls gathered together who were snickering about something. Then I noticed another girl off in the corner by herself, crying. I found out that the girl who was crying had become so nervous about going on stage that she had accidentally wet herself a little bit, and everyone could see a wet spot on her leotard. The group of laughing girls were talking about it and making fun of her. Can you imagine how awful she felt, not only that it happened, but also that people knew and were making fun of her instead of helping her figure out what to do about it?

The last type of bullying is *physical bullying*, which involves a person being physically beaten up or his or her things being broken or torn up. Physical bullying can include spitting on someone, tripping or pushing someone, hitting or kicking someone, breaking or taking someone's things, or even making rude or mean hand gestures at a person. Ask yourself these questions:

Has anyone ever taken something from you or broken something that you really liked?

Have you ever taken or broken something that belonged to someone else?

Have you ever been beaten up, or have you been the one who beat someone else up?

 Here's something I remember from growing up that I'll probably never forget. There was a boy in my sixth-grade class who was small for his age, and another boy who was older and a lot bigger and stronger. Not every day, but at least several times each week, the older boy would walk behind the smaller boy, tapping him on the back of the head with a piece of rolled-up paper and calling him a wimp over and over. Now, the tapping didn't hurt the boy—it was just a tube of paper, after all—but that very physical thing done over and over, combined with the name-calling, really made the smaller kid feel horrible. I'm glad he wasn't being beaten up, but it was still a kind of physical abuse.

All these things are bullying, especially when they happen more than once. Bullying is not a very nice thing to do!

Erainna Winnett, Ed. S.

BULLYING CAN HAPPEN ANYTIME, ANYWHERE

BULLYING CAN HAPPEN AT ANY time of day and on any day of the week. Most of the time, bullying happens during or after school hours, often right in the school building itself. It also can happen on the bus or playground and on the way to and from school. It can even happen in your own neighborhood. Bullying can also happen on the Internet, which is called cyberbullying. I'm going to talk about that in Chapter 2.

WHY ARE SOME PEOPLE BULLIES?

BOTH BOYS AND GIRLS CAN be bullies. There are all kinds of reasons that kids become bullies. Some of them just think it's funny and may not even realize they're hurting people (although some know *exactly* what they're doing). Sometimes they think it will make them fit in or seem cool to others. Some just think it's okay to be mean.

Some bullies may not think they're being mean at all. They think they're just being funny. Other people are laughing, so it must be funny, right? Picking on or being mean to someone is *never* funny, no matter what.

Do you think it's funny when someone hurts other people's feelings? What about when someone hurts yours?

Sometimes a bully thinks that picking on others will help him or her fit in better. The bully just wants to be liked and will do whatever he or she has to in order to be liked by a group.

Have you ever done something so that you would fit in with a group of kids? Did it involve hurting someone else?

Some kids don't know that it's *not okay* to hurt other people. Sometimes they may see other people doing it and feel as though it's okay for them to do it, too.

Have you ever seen someone hurting someone else? Did you think it was okay, or did you try to stop the person?

WHY DO SOME KIDS GET BULLIED MORE THAN OTHERS?

LOTS OF KIDS GET BULLIED, and they definitely *don't* deserve it. If you are being bullied by anyone, it's *not your fault*, and *you don't deserve it*, either. Remember that you can *always* ask for help from adults. You don't have to try and fix it all by yourself.

A bully likes to feel *powerful* and *in control*, right? So what do you think some of the things are that a bully will look for to feel better about him- or herself?

Bullies look for *differences*. Everyone is different or unique, and bullies know this. They look for the people who are different from them, whether it's their hair color, their clothes, their accent, or maybe even a disability such as being in a wheelchair or having a problem with speech. Please remember that *everyone* is different, and *everyone* still deserves to be treated nicely and with respect.

Do you know someone who is different from you? Are you nice to that person, or have you been mean to him or her in some way?

If you have been mean to someone because he or she is different from you, go apologize to that person and try to be friends instead. The person may not want to at first, but just keep being nice and see how it turns out.

I saw a really great example of this back when I was a fifth-grade science teacher. There was a girl who was really smart with science. She loved doing experiments and took all her science homework assignments really seriously. She was always raising her hand to answer questions, and she always gave the correct answers. Some of the other girls in class picked on her for being so into science, calling her a geek or a nerd and saying she was more interested in science than looking pretty (her hair was often a bit of a tangled mess). This constant mean treatment really had her feeling bad, even though I always encouraged and supported her in her love of science. We were about to start work on a big science project, and all the kids had to work with a partner. One of the boys in class who was very popular and also very good at science asked her if she would be his partner. I remember her asking him, "Why would *you* want to work with *me?*" He just smiled and said, "Because you and I are the best ones at science, so I think we'd make a great team." And they *did* make a great team. He became a good friend to her, which was exactly what she needed.

Bullies also look for someone who is an *easy target.* Bullies don't just pick on or hurt someone because he or she is different. They look for people who are *easy* to hurt. Maybe the person is smaller or doesn't have as many friends as someone else. One thing you need to remember is that you *do* have the right to *be yourself,* and no one has the right to harm or hurt you. Everyone deserves respect. If you or someone you know is being bullied, ask your parents or another adult about the laws about bullying where you live. Everyone has rights.

Bullies are also more likely to bully kids who don't speak up and tell adults what's going on. Kids who bully tend to do it when no one else is around to see it or tell on them. If you see someone being bullied, or if you're the one being bullied, you should talk to an adult. You can always talk to your parents about it first, but if you don't want to talk to your parents, talk to a teacher or adult at school who you know and trust. If that adult doesn't do anything about it, find another adult who will. Everyone can speak up and be protected from being bullied. If you ever experience bullying or see it happening, who will you talk to? Make a list of adults you know and trust below:

_____

_____

_____

DON'T MAKE BULLYING WORSE!

THERE ARE THINGS THAT DON'T help bullying, like fighting back or not doing anything.

You may be tempted to put on your superhero costume and save the day, but trying to fight back or get even with a bully *never* works. When you fight back, there is a good chance that the bullying will keep happening, and it may even get worse. Fighting back can also get you into trouble, especially if people mistakenly think *you're* the one being a bully.

Another bad idea is just sitting back and doing nothing. You may think the bullying will stop if you look the other way and don't say anything, but that just isn't true. The truth is, when you ignore a problem like bullying, it will only get worse.

HOW CAN YOU STOP BULLYING?

IF YOU SEE SOMEONE WHO is being bullied or you are the one being bullied, you can feel pretty helpless. You may think there's nothing you can do to stop it, but the good news is that there are things you can do! Remember, though, that it's not all up to you. Get other people involved. Every step, no matter how small, can make a real difference.

As I mentioned before, you can go to a trusted adult and tell him or her about the bullying. Look back at your list of five adults you know and trust. If the first one doesn't do anything, try the next one. Keep telling adults about it until someone does something.

There are other things you can do as well. You can ask the bully to stop. The bully may not realize that what he or she is doing is hurtful to the other person. He or she may just think it's funny. You *must not* join in. A bully often does the bullying when he or she has an audience. If the bully sees that no one is watching or joining in, he or she may get the message that it's not cool and stop doing it.

 You can also be a good friend to a person who is being bullied. Walk with that person to class, play with him or her at recess, and let the person know that he or she is not alone and doesn't have to put up with the bullying. Tell the person that he or she can do something about it. Many times, kids who are being bullied think that they have said or done something to deserve it. This simply isn't true! Everyone, no matter who they are, deserves respect and safety. It is *never* okay to bully or be bullied. No one deserves to have someone be mean to them.

Ask your friends to stand up with you against the bullying. When everyone sticks together, it makes a big difference! Make a list of *five friends* you can ask to help you stop bullying in your school or community:

_____

_____

_____

_____

_____

Now that you've made your list, go to each person and ask him or her to sign a petition *against* bullying. Challenge those friends to find five of their own friends to sign the petition. Pretty soon, your *whole school* will know about it and be willing to stand up against bullying.

Even though bullying is a big problem in schools and communities, there are still lots of people who don't know much about it. Talk to a teacher or your school principal about getting a program to educate everyone about bullying and what can be done to stop it. Learning about it is the first step!

Every small step to stop bullying helps. Yes, even YOU can make a huge difference in the way others are treated. But you don't have to do it all by yourself. Ask others to help you!

CHAPTER 2: CYBERBULLYING—WHEN BULLIES GO ONLINE

WHAT IN THE WORLD IS CYBERBULLYING?

IT SEEMS AS THOUGH BULLIES have been around forever, but with the Internet, bullying has been taken to a whole new level. Cyberbullying involves being threatened, harassed, embarrassed, tormented, humiliated, or targeted in a mean way by another person through the Internet, on mobile phones, or using any other digital technology.

The ways that cyberbullies can do this are practically unlimited. The cyberbully can also be a bully one minute and a victim the very next minute. These roles can switch from bully to victim and back again. There have even been times when children have hurt each other or themselves after being involved in cyberbullying, so it's something we have to take very seriously.

ARE YOU A CYBERBULLY?

CYBERBULLYING IS SO EASY TO do that it can happen before you even know what you've really done. But before you start feeling bad about yourself, take the quiz below to see if you might be part of the problem.

For each of the things listed, give yourself a score depending on if or how often you've done it, where **0** means you've never done it, **1** means you've done it once or twice, **2** means you've done it three to five times, and **3** means you've done it more than five times. For each of the statements below, you'll see a blank line where you can write the score you're giving yourself.

Signed on using someone else's screen name to get information _____

Sent an email from someone else's account _____

Pretended to be someone else online or through texting _____

Teased or scared someone through texting _____

Posted information or pictures about someone without his or her permission _____

Used information you found online to embarrass, harass, or tease someone _____

Sent scary or rude things to someone online, even just joking _____

Used bad words online _____

Forwarded pictures of someone without his or her knowledge or permission _____

Posted rude or untrue things about someone online _____

Used someone else's password without his or her permission _____

Add up your score and write it here: _____

If you got anywhere from 0 to 4 points, you are a cybersaint, meaning your behavior online is ideal. Keep it up!

If you got between 5 and 9 points, you're definitely not perfect, but very few people are. You probably haven't done anything too bad and were just trying to have fun. Try not to do stuff like that again, because it is hurtful to others. Keep in mind that though it's fun for you, it could be causing other people pain.

If you got from 10 to 16 points, you are a cybersinner, and your behavior online definitely needs some major improvements. You have done too many dangerous, punishable, and wrong things online, and you need to work to clean up your cyber-record.

If you got more than 16 points, you are definitely a cyberbully. You need to turn your behavior around right away because you are headed in a very bad direction. You need to sign off from all technology and think about what you have done before something serious happens to you or someone else, if it hasn't already.

WHY DO KIDS BECOME CYBERBULLIES?

WHEN IT COMES TO CYBERBULLYING, kids are usually doing it because they don't know how to deal with their feelings of revenge, frustration, or anger. Sometimes they do it because they are bored and have too much spare time and easy access to technology. Others may do it for entertainment, laughs, or to get a reaction out of others. Sometimes people even do it accidentally, either sending a message before they think it through or sending it to the wrong person by mistake.

Since there are different reasons people do it, we have to use different ways of solving the problem. There is no "one size fits all" way to stop it.

After reading about the reasons that people cyberbully, do you see yourself or someone you know falling into any of those categories? If you do, get help immediately from a trusted adult. You don't want it to get worse!

RULES FOR ONLINE COMMUNICATIONS

BEFORE YOU HIT SEND ON that email or text, or post on a social network site, you need to go back over what you are planning to send. If it matches any of the numbered points below, fix them before you send it. If you can't fix them, don't send it. Online messages can be easily misunderstood. That's why we all have to be really careful to make them clear and help others understand what we mean so we don't hurt anyone.

1. **Make sure you are sending the message to the right place so the right person receives it.** Double-check the spelling of the screen name. Is the person already in your  address book or your buddy list? When someone sends you something, you should make sure that his or her screen name is saved to your list so you always have the right one. Just because you send it doesn't mean that the person receives it!

   So, when you send something and don't get a reply, don't get mad! Ask the person if he or she received it. Also, don't send something to someone if you would be embarrassed by his or her parents or older siblings reading it first. Many families use shared screen names and email accounts.

2. **Make sure it is something that is worth sending.** Don't send rumors! If you don't have anything good to say, don't say anything at all.

3. **Before you hit send, make sure you proofread and spell-check your emails, and make sure to identify yourself so the person getting it knows who you are.** Messages are often misunderstood

because words are left out, or things aren't said clearly, or there are misspelled words. Emails don't have to be perfect, but they do need to be clear! If your words 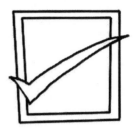 are important enough to send, they are important enough to be understood, right? The rules for texting are a little different because spelling and grammar mistakes are more common and accepted there than they are in email messages. Always reread your message before sending it to make sure you are saying what you want to say. If it could be understood in two different ways, either reword it or use one of those little emoticon faces to let the other person know what you mean. Don't use a bunch of abbreviations or shortened words that he or she won't understand. If you are talking about someone else, make sure that's very clear to the person receiving your message!

 Here is something that happened to a student in my school recently. Auditions were being held for the spring play, which was going to be a musical, so everyone had to sing during their audition, even if they didn't want a big part.

terrible singer, and so is the music teacher."
Her friend thought she was saying that the
music teacher was a terrible singer! That's
not what she meant. She meant that she
thought the music teacher was probably
also glad she didn't do well at the audition,
knowing how nervous she would be if they
gave her a big part. Can you see how easy
it is for an email message to say something
you really didn't mean if you aren't clear?

Always sign your emails with a name that the
person who is getting it knows, especially if your
username is different from your real name. Don't
give out any personal information, but letting the
other person know that you are using a different
screen name helps your message be read instead
of marked as spam. It helps if you put that
information in the subject line.

4. **Make sure you're not angry when you
   write the message.** If you write a message
   when you're angry, review it carefully and
   then take time to cool off before you send
   it. If someone sends you something that is
   meant to insult you or harass you, ignore
   it. This will make it go away much faster
   because the person who sent it is probably
   trying on purpose to get a reaction out of

you. If you don't react, he or she will get bored and go away.

Can you think of any other rules for online behavior? List them below:

_____

_____

_____

_____

HOW TO DEAL WITH CYBERBULLIES

LEARNING ABOUT CYBERBULLYING IS THE first step in preventing and learning how to deal with it. Talk to trusted adults about starting a campaign in your school or community to help with the problem of cyberbullying. You can learn how to avoid becoming a cyberbully, how to stop cyberbullying, and how to be accountable for your own actions.

When you do come across a cyberbully online, learn to **take five**, which means walking away from the computer or other device for at least five minutes and finding something else to do that will help you calm down. You can go for a walk or run, do some deep-breathing exercises or yoga, or do whatever else might relax you. Do whatever you need to do in order to avoid becoming a cyberbully. You need to know that you can get into really big trouble with the police or even the FBI for cyberbullying.

I've already told you how mean words can cause other people a lot of hurt, and that's the most common kind of hurt caused by cyberbullying. Sometimes people who are being cyberbullied get so upset that they end up attacking the bully or hurting themselves to make it stop.

If you or someone you know is being cyberbullied online, contact a trusted adult. If you know someone who is doing it, let the person know that *it is not okay* and that you will tell on him or her. Silence is never acceptable, especially when others are being hurt!

Also, you can block the cyberbully from being able to contact you, so make sure you find a trusted adult who can help make that happen. But be sure you save all the bad messages and forward them to your Internet service provider (ISP) so they can investigate the bullying. You can also show those messages to your trusted adult so he or she knows exactly what is going on and who is doing it.

There is help for you if you are being cyberbullied. Just be brave, be smart, and take action!

You can help stop cyberbullying by refusing to pass on messages that are hurtful to others. Get your friends to help you stop cyberbullying by blocking communication with the cyberbullies and reporting them to trusted adults. Keep yourself safe online! You should never share or post your personal information or your friends' personal information online, meaning your full name, parents' names, address, phone number, the name of your school, or your parents' credit card information. You should also never share your passwords with anyone, no matter how much you think you can trust them. Finally, never *ever* agree to meet someone in person that you've met online!

RULES FOR SAFE SOCIAL SITES

YOU PROBABLY KNOW HOW SOCIAL media sites such as Facebook and Twitter are super popular, especially with kids your age. But the big question is, how can you enjoy these fun sites and still play it safe? Here are some tips I want you to know about:

1. **Never fill out any information that would lead bad people to find you.** Don't give out your information to anyone online, no matter what! Someone may say that he or she is your friend from math class, but the person may not actually know you at all.

2. **Have your parents check your privacy settings on your social media accounts** to make sure they are set so that no information is shown to people you are not friends with. Only your name will show.

3. **Ask your parents before uploading any pictures to social media sites.** Have your parents change the settings so they have to approve pictures that other people "tag" you with before they are posted. Your parents or other trusted adults should have the right to remove anything from your page that is inappropriate or could be seen as offensive to others.

4. **Only be friends online with people you know in real life.** Also, make sure you are friends with your parents or another adult you can trust on these social media sites so he or she can keep an eye on you and who is talking to you. That way, bad people won't be as likely to bother you, or if they do, it can be stopped. Also, this will keep other people from being mean to you and help you not be mean to others. Why would you want to be online friends with someone you don't even really know?

5. **Remember that what you do online is there FOREVER.** It never goes away. That is why it is very important that you always

be nice and don't post things that you wouldn't want to come up later on. When you get older and want to start working, you don't want people to know that you were an online bully when you were younger, do you? Being mean online is a little different from being mean in person. When you're mean to someone in person, you can see right away the hurt that you cause him or her. When you're mean online, you may never even know the hurt you have caused to the way the person feels about him- or herself. Also, you may type something meant as a joke, but the other person may not realize that, so make sure you make your meaning clear by using the fun emoticons. Little smiley faces let people know that you're kidding!

You can delete something and make it go away for now, but someone else may have saved it or downloaded it. He or she might decide to use it later on to hurt you.

6. **Don't answer personal questions online.** You've seen those online questions that ask things like *Mom's name?* or *Dad's name?* or even *Shoe size?* and so on. Don't answer those personal questions online! Many times, bad people will try to use them to get your information and then use it to hurt you in some way. Think about

it before you post it! Ask yourself: "Could someone find me and hurt me if I answer this question?" If the answer is yes, don't answer it!

I know it's hard to believe, but there really are bad people out there who want to hurt great kids like you. Giving out your personal information online is one way they try to find you, so never do it!

7. **Just like talking to someone face-to-face, you should never type anything on the computer when you're mad.** When you're mad, you might say things that you don't really mean, but they come out anyway because of how you feel in the moment. If someone puts something mean about you online and you find it, log off the computer and *take five*—walk away for five minutes or longer. Later on, you can go back and email the person or talk face-to-face and let him or her know that what he or she said about you was very hurtful. Maybe the person will take it back. Whatever happens, don't try to get even by finding some way to hurt him or her in return. Just move on.

Can you think of some other rules for staying safe online?

_____

_____

_____

_____

CELL PHONE RULES

 Like social media sites, it's pretty common for kids your age to have cell phones. You must learn how to be responsible with them in order to enjoy having one. Most cell phones these days have cameras. You should be smart about what pictures you take and who you send them to.

1. **NEVER take pictures of yourself without any clothes on or send those kinds of pictures to anyone.** Another person can use this later on to hurt you, or a photo could end up in the hands of a bad person who might use it to do bad things. Just as with online sites, there are bad people out there who want to hurt kids like you.

2. **When you're in the locker room for gym class or you're at the local gym, don't take pictures of other people without their clothes on.**  That could get you into really big trouble! Plus, you don't want to hurt anyone, do you? You should never take pictures or send pictures of anyone without the person knowing about it and agreeing to it first. You wouldn't want people to do that to you, would you? You shouldn't do it, either.

3. **Only give your cell phone number to your friends and other people that your parents or trusted adult say it's okay to give it to.** Don't go around giving your phone number to anyone and everyone who wants it. There's no reason to give it to that guy who was trying to talk to you at the grocery store while your mom was shopping.

4. **Don't send mean text messages to people.** If it's not something you would say to someone's face, you shouldn't say it in a text message, either—whether you send it to that person or someone else. If you send it to someone else, there is still a chance that the person will end up seeing

it. If you can't text anything nice, don't text anything at all!

Can you think of more tips that could help keep you safe and responsible while using your cell phone?

Cyberbullying is a big problem these days. It doesn't just take place online or on social media sites like Facebook and Twitter; it can also happen on cell phones. You should never be mean to anyone—either directly to their face, online, or through a cell phone. Always be careful what you say! You could hurt someone's feelings without even realizing it. If you have something to say that might potentially hurt someone, make sure to use the emoticon smiley face to let the person know you're just joking!

CHAPTER 3: PONDERING PEER PRESSURE

DO YOU KNOW ABOUT PEER PRESSURE?

As you grow up, you are going to be faced with all kinds of challenging choices. Some of them don't have a right or wrong answer, like what sport to play or what clubs to join. But some choices can and will involve serious things such as skipping class; trying cigarettes, drugs, or alcohol; and even lying to your parents.

Trying to make choices by yourself is hard enough, but it can be even harder when other people are around and trying to get you to do something. People who are the same age as you, such as the kids in your class, are called your peers. When they try to pressure you to do something or act a certain way, it is called peer pressure. Everyone (even grownups) has to deal with peer pressure. Think about answers to these questions:

Have you ever had to deal with peer pressure?

What did you do to deal with it?

WHAT EXACTLY IS PEER PRESSURE?

YOUR PEERS REALLY DO AFFECT your life and your choices, even if you don't notice it. This happens simply by spending time with each other. You learn from each other, and it's only natural for you to want to listen to and learn from the friends you spend time with. After all, you want to fit in and be liked, right? Peer pressure can be both positive and negative.

Peer pressure can be negative, such as a friend trying to get you to skip class with him or her, or a friend trying to get you to bully someone or even shoplift. Think about it:

*Have any of your friends ever tried to get you to do anything that you **know** is wrong? Did you do it?*

 Peer pressure can also be positive. Maybe a classmate taught you a neat memory device to remember the names of the planets, or you learned a neat trick with a soccer ball. You may want to be like your friend who is really good at sports. Maybe you just read a book and really liked it, and now others want to read it, too.

Have any of your friends ever tried to get you to do something positive? Have you tried to get your friends to do something positive?

WHY DO PEOPLE GIVE IN TO PEER PRESSURE?

SOMETIMES YOU MAY GIVE IN to peer pressure because you want to fit in or you want to be liked. Or maybe you're afraid that other kids may pick on you or laugh at you if you *don't* go along with the group. Sometimes you may just be curious about what they are doing and want to try it out for yourself. If you ever find yourself thinking "Well, everyone is doing it," you may give in more easily yourself.

When have you ever given in to peer pressure?

Was it positive or negative?

Did you feel good about it afterward?

If you start feeling peer pressure, you should stop and ask yourself some questions like these:

✓   Could this get me in trouble? Will it be breaking any rules or, even worse, the law?

✓   Will my parents be mad at me if I do this?

✓   Will others who are in authority be mad or disappointed with me?

✓   Will someone be hurt in some way?

✓   Do I feel good about doing this?

HOW TO DEAL WITH NEGATIVE PEER PRESSURE

 As you get older, you'll experience more and more peer pressure, and the negative peer pressure will get riskier. You'll be better off if you learn how to deal with it now. Here are some tips on how to deal with negative peer pressure.

1. **Just say NO!** Set limits with your peers. Let them know that there are some things

you simply will not do, no matter what they say or do to try to convince you. You can suggest something else, change the subject, or simply walk away. Some ways you can say no are:

✓ Simply say "NO!"

✓ Make an excuse and leave, or simply walk away.

✓ Change the subject and don't let them change it back.

✓ Laugh and then change the subject or leave.

✓ Offer friendly advice such as "C'mon, you're too smart for that!"

✓ Say "You're entitled to your opinion, and I'm entitled to mine."

However you decide to say no, say it quickly and firmly. Be sure your peers know that your mind is made up and you're not going to talk about it anymore. Believe it or not, if you're not used to saying no in these ways, you may need to actually practice doing it!

One piece of advice, though: Saying no to your teacher every time you're asked to do something is not a good way to practice saying no! That's more likely to get you in trouble than anything else. I remember once that I had spent time with a group of fourth graders and told them how to "just say no." Later, at the end of class, the teacher told all the kids to line up quietly at the door to get ready for lunch. One little boy immediately shouted out "No!" The teacher asked, "Why would you say that?" And the boy replied, "I'm practicing saying no!" The teacher looked at me as if to say, "Great. This is what I'm going to have to deal with for the rest of the day!"

Write out a statement saying NO to negative peer pressure. Then practice saying it in front of a mirror.

_____

_____

_____

2. **Choose better friends**—the kind that you know won't try to get you to do something that you shouldn't do. If one of your friends does try to get you to do something wrong, tell the person that if he or she is going to act like that, you can't stay friends. Let that person know you like being friends and want to stay friends, but you can't be doing things that are bad.

Make a list of five friends who are good for you because they don't ask you to do things you shouldn't. You want more friends like these!

1

_____

2

_____

3

_____

4

_____

5

_____

3. **Make good choices.** Think about the ways a situation could turn out *before* you get into it. Think it through and listen to your heart *and* head. Together, they will almost always point you in the right direction. Pay attention to what your parents and other adults in your life say are good choices. Never make a quick decision based on trying to fit in with your friends!

4. **Value yourself.** You are a good, smart person, and you deserve the best, right? So don't let your friends drag you down by

getting you to do bad things. Find things to do that you enjoy and that you are good at, and only have friends who want to do the same. Taking this approach will make you stronger and make it much harder for someone else to influence you to do bad things.

Make a list of five things you are good at:

1

___

2

___

3

___

4

___

5

___

Talk to some adults about peer pressure, especially if you're dealing with it now. They can help you with some ideas about what you should and shouldn't do. If possible, it's best to go talk to your parents as soon as a friend tries to pressure you to do something, even though you may not feel like doing that.

Make a list of five adults you can go talk to when peer pressure comes up:

1

_____

2

_____

3

_____

4

_____

5

_____

WHAT DOES PEER PRESSURE DO TO YOU?

Peer Pressure can affect you in some negative ways, like the ones below:

- You don't think of the consequences.

- You do what others want you to do.

- You join in the trouble and start telling lies.

- You use negative peer pressure and leave others out.

- You become someone who isn't trusted or respected.

Peer pressure can also affect you in some good, positive ways:

- You learn to stop and think first.

- You learn to make good choices.

- You learn to take action to avoid trouble.

- You use positive peer pressure.

- You become someone who is trusted and respected.

YOU CAN FEEL NEGATIVE PEER PRESSURE

 WHEN YOU ARE BEING PRESSURED to do something *bad*, that is what we call *negative* peer pressure. Your body will react to the negative peer pressure, and you will begin to feel afraid. How do you know you are starting to feel afraid? Your body will tell you with the signs below:

- Your mouth will feel dry.

- Your legs will begin to feel shaky.

- Your heart will beat faster, and you'll get that "butterflies in your tummy" feeling.

- Your head might feel hot or cold.

These are the same kinds of feelings you might get in other situations—like when you're standing in line to go on a really wild ride at an amusement park and you're a little scared or nervous about it. You might also get that same feeling just before you're about to run a race or go on stage for a performance.

These are just a few of the things your body will do when you are pressured to do something that you know in your heart is wrong. Can you think of any others? What are some things your body does when you start feeling afraid? Write them down below:

_____

_____

_____

POSITIVE PEER PRESSURE

ALL THIS TALK ABOUT NEGATIVE peer pressure may leave you feeling pretty scared! You don't have to be afraid, because not all peer pressure is hurtful. *Positive* peer pressure does exist, like when you help your friends or they help you with homework, or you support each other in standing up against alcohol or drugs. You can make your own choices and stand up for what you think is right, especially if you know that your friends, parents, and other trusted adults are there to support you!

Positive peer pressure can also be called *peer support*. This means using your friendships to help and support each other in all kinds of ways, like the ones below:

- You learn to set limits such as no gossiping or bullying.

- You learn to help each other make good choices.

- You learn to accept each other's differences because everyone is different, so why not embrace it?

- You learn to get involved together in positive activities such as friendships, music, and sports.

- You are able to join other positive people in groups such as sports teams, scouts, drama, and other fun groups or clubs.

Being part of a group of positive peers can offer great things such as the following:

- You feel valued and part of a group.

- You feel confident and secure with those who share your interests and values.

- You know that you can take positive risks and offer your ideas without being bullied or judged.

- You get to know more people and learn about their thoughts and ideas.

- You learn to get along with others and make decisions.

- You share interests and learn new things from others.

- You feel as though you are accepted and listened to.

ALL THE THINGS PEER PRESSURE CAN DO TO YOU

WHEN YOU GIVE IN TO negative peer pressure, you end up with several bad results.

When you do something that doesn't match up with your values and morals because of giving in to peer pressure, you will probably feel guilty about it. You may feel as though you let down your parents or other adults and feel really bad about it.

When you give in to peer pressure all the time to keep everyone else happy, you end up kind of losing yourself. You don't know how to do what makes *you* happy anymore—only what makes *others* happy. This can also make you feel like not bothering to make good and right decisions, which means that you will start depending on others to make decisions for you. You can get to the point where you don't even know what *your* favorite music, clothes, or movies are because you're only doing what everyone else is doing!

 *EVERYONE*—**even you**—will face peer pressure at some point in your life and probably a lot more than just once. It could be now, or it could be later on in life, but it will come.

You need to understand that not all peer pressure is bad. Sometimes it can be a good thing if it encourages you and makes you feel good about yourself and what you are doing.

Positive peer pressure can help you become a better student and an all-around better person. Positive peer pressure can help you put a stop to bullying. Negative peer pressure can and will bring you down. You can lose yourself if you fall into the trap of negative peer pressure. You may end up doing drugs or, worse, ending up in jail later on in life. When it comes to negative peer pressure, learn how to say **no** and mean it!

CHAPTER 4: GETTING CLEAR ON CLIQUES

WHAT IN THE WORLD IS A CLIQUE?

A *CLIQUE* IS *NOT* SOMETHING you do on the computer with a mouse. That's *click*, although *clique* is pronounced the same way. A *clique* is a group of kids who are excluding others from being part of their group.

You should have friends you can connect with and who have the same or similar interests as you. It will make you more confident and secure, and you will feel as though you are part of something.

Groups of friends are not a problem until you start leaving people out or acting mean to people who are not in your group of friends. That's when your group of friends becomes a *clique.*

Cliques are typically very tight groups with a leader who tells you what to do and how you can act. The leader might even tell you who you can and can't be friends with. He or she is often rude or mean to other people. Though you may think it's better to be part of a clique than be left out, you need to understand that you'll be under a lot more pressure and have to follow a large number of rules. You may find yourself worrying a lot that you'll say or do the wrong thing and end up being excluded or becoming the target of their meanness.

Is your group of friends open to people who are different or have different interests than you? Does the group leave people out on purpose?

BUT WHAT IF YOU REALLY DON'T FIT IN?

FEELING AS THOUGH YOU DON'T fit in anywhere is a big deal. Lots of people feel this way, no matter what age they are. You can feel hurt and confused wondering why you don't fit in. It would be so much better if the solution were as simple as being more outgoing in getting to know others. But the real issue behind this comes down to how YOU feel about it. You are in control of your thoughts and feelings, and you can make changes. First you have to become aware of those thoughts that are telling you that you don't fit in. Here are a few questions to ask yourself to figure out some of the common thoughts that are causing you to feel this way:

1. What does "fitting in" mean to you? Different people have different meanings for "fitting in." So, what exactly does it mean for YOU? Check off as many of the statements below as fit for you.

   ___ Being the center of attention

   ___ People coming to you to talk to you or hang out

   ___ Having lots of friends

   ___ Feeling as though you're an important part of the group

   ___ People wanting to know what you think about things

2. Do you start conversations, or do you wait for others to start talking to you?

3. Do you think there is a wall between you and others?

4. Are you afraid of being hurt or put down by others?

5. Do you appreciate and like yourself?

By answering these questions, you'll see if it is your thoughts and feelings that are making you feel as though you don't fit in. Don't let your own thoughts get in the way of becoming friends with people. You *are* a wonderful person. Anyone would be lucky to be friends with you!

WHY DO PEOPLE JOIN CLIQUES?

PEOPLE JOIN CLIQUES FOR DIFFERENT reasons. In some cases, being cool or popular is the most important thing, and the clique gives them that. Others want to be in cliques because they don't like being left out. Some think it's better to be part of the clique than not, which is *not* true.

Cliques give people who like to be in control the chance to do that, for better or worse. For those who are more comfortable being a follower, it gives them clear rules to learn and follow. It is usually made very clear to those who are in the clique what they have to do to fit in. In some cases, this means you have to give up your freedom and follow someone else rather than doing what *you* want or feel is right.

When you're in a clique, you are being controlled by the leaders, who have the power to decide who is and isn't part of the clique. This type of control especially happens in girl cliques. Just because you're popular and likeable doesn't mean you'll be allowed in the clique. The leader might not like it if you're confident or have a great personality. You also might not like being a follower, especially if you have enough friends on your own. Your friends may be invited to join the clique, but you may be left out.

Girls aren't the only ones who form cliques. Boys do it too, often around a computer game, certain music, or sports. Boys can be just as mean to those outside the clique as girls can.

CLIQUES MAKE PEOPLE FEEL LEFT OUT

If you are not part of a clique, you can feel quite confused and frustrated. Maybe someone was your best friend last week, and now he or she is being mean to you and doesn't want to sit with you at lunch. You may be sad or angry, or even feel like crying. You may be scared that someone may try to pick on you or start a fight with you. You probably feel hurt that you are being left out.

Sometimes the kids in a clique may feel bad about the way they are treating others, but they can't figure out how they can be nice to people *outside* the clique and still be considered cool by the kids *in* the clique. This is not a good excuse, though. Lots of kids are able to be nice to everyone, both in and out of their closest group of friends, without being part of a clique.

Have you ever been left out? How did it make you feel?

Have you ever left someone out? How do you think it made him or her feel?

GETTING OUT OF A CLIQUE

Maybe you are in a clique, and you really don't want to be part of it anymore. You don't want to leave others out anymore and hurt their feelings. Maybe you see that you are missing out on being great friends with people outside your clique.

Maybe you're just tired of being told what to do and who to talk to, and you don't want someone else to be in charge of you, or you are afraid that your "friends" will start making fun of you or being mean to you. Maybe something mean was said about someone you care about.

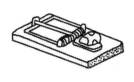 If you feel as though you're trapped in a clique and you're ready to get out, you can do it! You can take the following steps:

1. Make some friends outside your clique so you don't feel lonely when you leave your clique behind. You will want to make friends with people who will be respectful and accepting of others, no matter what their differences are. Avoid being friends with people who are mean to others or who only think of themselves.

2. Find things to do outside the clique and school. Think about doing some community theater or getting involved in a sport. When you focus your time and energy on your own activities, you learn exactly how *unimportant* cliques really are. You can be friends with a lot of different kinds of people and do a lot of different fun things. You don't have to hang out with the same people all the time.

3. Make sure you pull away carefully, without actually telling them "I'm leaving." Start by just spending less time with them. If there are any people in the clique that you are close to and want to stay friends with, get them to come with you. As long as you don't make it obvious that you are leaving, you might be able to avoid a lot of drama later on, especially from the leaders of the clique. If people say anything about you leaving the clique, tell them how you feel about the way they treat others. Maybe if they hear your views, they will change theirs.

4. Be open and honest about how you feel to someone you can trust as you leave the clique. You may be worried that you won't be able to find new friends or be popular anymore. Talk to a parent, counselor, or someone else you can trust so you can explain these feelings to that person and even get his or her advice.

Have you ever had to leave your group of friends? How did it make you feel?

PLAYGROUND POLITICS, PART I

RECESS IS ONE PLACE WHERE I see a lot of cliques forming. Deciding who to play with can be a tough choice to make, especially if you feel pressured to play with a particular kid or group of kids every day. You know in your head that you should play with more than just the same kids all the time, but doing it feels hard. When I was a playground monitor, I remember seeing a girl sitting by herself and looking a little bit sad. When I asked her what was wrong, she said she didn't have anyone to play with. I looked around at a playground full of children playing and laughing, and I said it looked as though there were lots of kids to play with. But then she said how playing with one group would make another group mad. I told her that *not* making a choice didn't look like a very fun solution. I suggested she tell the one group that she would play with them tomorrow and then go ahead and play with the other group. It was as if she didn't realize she really could stand up for herself and make a choice! She ended up having a great time with one group that day and a fun time with the other group the next day.

STANDING UP FOR YOU

IN ORDER TO STAND UP for yourself, you first need to make the change. If you are tired of being a people pleaser or being pushed around, you are ready to get started. You need to change how others see you and how you interact with them.

To start standing up for yourself, you need to believe in yourself. If you are not confident, you will have trouble succeeding in anything. People won't look up to you if you don't have self-confidence. It's easy to see when someone isn't confident in themselves or their abilities.

When someone is confident, it is obvious. People are less likely to pick on or tease someone who is confident.

Build your confidence by writing down a few things you are good at:

_____

_____

_____

_____

The next step is to make a change in your *attitude*. Attitude is everything; it shows others who you are through the signals you send. You show your attitude in the tone of your voice, your body language, your facial expressions, and even your thoughts. Attitude is contagious! If you have a good attitude about things, you will be an encouragement to those around you to feel good about themselves. Decide that you're going to have a good attitude and you'll be well on your way to standing up for yourself.

Finally, you must think about the bad things that have happened to you that have caused you to **not** stand up for yourself. Everyone gets hurt, but what really matters is how you *respond* to the hurt. When you take the bad things personally and start avoiding things, you stop being able to stand up for yourself, and you let the bad parts of life get the best of you. You must decide to stop taking things so personally, but you may need some help from a trusted adult to help you work through your feelings and turn things around.

You may think that being part of a clique is cool. Being in a really close group of friends can feel awesome. This doesn't become a problem until the group starts leaving people out or being mean to them. If you find you've become a part of a clique, you might want to think about getting out of it and finding some friends who are respectful and accepting of others and their differences. You really can be friends with lots of different people and help others feel respected and accepted!

CHAPTER 5: CURING CONFLICTS

WHAT EXACTLY IS CONFLICT RESOLUTION?

SOMETIMES THINGS HAPPEN THAT MAKE you angry. You may feel as though something is unfair, or maybe something of yours was broken or taken from you, or a similar situation. Getting angry or upset isn't the problem. We all get angry and upset, but it's what you *do* when you get angry—how you *respond* to your anger or frustration—that shows whether or not there is a problem.

Erainna Winnett, Ed. S.

WHAT HAPPENS WHEN YOU GET ANGRY?

Do you throw a temper tantrum? Do you act mean to everyone around you? Can you see how that almost never solves the problem? What are some things you could do instead?

Well, you could take the time to use *conflict resolution*. When you do that, everything will be fair, and everyone will get something they want. There are four steps to conflict resolution:

1. Understanding the problem.

2. Avoiding making the problem worse.

3. Working together.

4. Finding a solution to the problem.

FINDING OUT WHAT THE PROBLEM REALLY IS

Everyone who is a part of the conflict needs to be understood. You have to take time to understand what exactly the conflict or argument is about. In order to understand what is going on, try the following:

1. Say what you feel about the conflict, hopefully without being interrupted.

72

2. Listen to what the other person or people have to say, and listen without interrupting them!

3. Put yourself in the other person's shoes and try to really understand what he or she is feeling.

Have you ever had a conflict in which you took the time to talk it over calmly and understand the real cause of the problem? Didn't that work better than fighting about it? It almost always does!

HOW TO NOT MAKE THE PROBLEM EVEN WORSE

IT CAN BE HARD, BUT when you are in an argument about something, you must remember to take some deep breaths and avoid making things worse than they already are. You can do this by trying out the following:

1. Avoid putting down the other person.

2. Refrain from making mean comments that will hurt his or her feelings. This means not making comments about the way the person looks and not bringing up things that may have happened in the past or any "secrets" he or she may have.

3. Screaming and shouting at the other person *never* help!

4. Never fight, kick, hit, push, or do anything else that would physically hurt the other person.

Can you think of anything else you can do or not do to keep from making things worse than they already are?

_____

_____

_____

_____

HOW WORKING TOGETHER CAN HELP

CONSIDER WORKING TOGETHER TO FIND a solution. It helps to make "I" statements that include the following:

1. I FEEL hurt when ...

2. I NEED to feel or be ...

3. I HEAR what you are saying, but I FEEL ...

There are also some things you should never say, like the following:

1. You ALWAYS ...

2. You NEVER ...

By saying things like the first three examples and not saying things like the last two, you are taking ownership of your feelings and needs, and you're not attacking the other person by blaming him or her. It is much better to say something like "I feel sad when you shout at me" than to say "You're always shouting at me!"

This step helps you take turns when you're talking. It might even help to set a time limit for each person to talk before you begin. This helps everyone have a chance to say what he or she wants and be heard and respected.

It can be really hard to keep your voice calm and not shout when you're angry, but a quiet, firm voice is much better. A loud, mean voice only causes everyone else to get upset, and then they won't be willing to really listen to what you are saying.

Each of you can write down what you think the problem is really about. Then trade your papers and read what the other person has written. Don't get defensive or upset—just read and be willing to understand.

Here are some things you can do to practice listening:

1. Look at the other person when he or she is talking in order to show that you're giving your full attention, but don't stare. Staring makes people uncomfortable.

2. Make "listening noises," but don't interrupt. Say "uh-huh," "yes," or "no" in the right places while the other person is talking. This lets him or her know that you really are listening to what he or she is saying.

3. Try repeating back what you heard the other person say, but only after he or she is finished talking. This gives the other person a chance to see if you heard what he or she was saying.

Can you think of anything else that would help you to work together to understand each other?

_____

_____

_____

_____

_____

FINDING A SOLUTION TO THE PROBLEM

ONCE YOU'VE TAKEN THE TIME to listen and understand each other and everyone understands exactly what the problem is, it is time to find a solution. You can do this by trying out the following:

1. Brainstorm together to think of ways to work out the problem. Think of as many ways as you can, even if they seem silly at first. Sometimes those solutions work the best!

2. Ask another person to write down your ideas as you say them, or maybe come up with ways to help your ideas work so the conflict can be resolved quickly.

Can you think of other ways to find solutions to the problem?

POSSIBLE DIFFERENT ENDINGS TO THE CONFLICT

There are three possible outcomes to the conflict resolution process:

✓ **Win/Win.** Everyone involved is happy with the way things worked out.

✓ **Win/Lose.** One of you is happy because you got exactly what you wanted, and the other person is not happy because he or she did not get what he or she wanted.

✓ **Lose/Lose.** Neither of you are happy because neither of you got what you wanted. Maybe your parents stepped in because you couldn't work it out between yourselves, so now neither of you got anything.

Of course, the best one is Win/Win because everyone involved in the conflict gets at least part of what they wanted. You will have to get really good at conflict resolution to be sure that everyone gets what he or she wants.

If you can't work things out between yourselves, you may want to get a trusted adult or another person, sometimes called a *peer mediator*, involved to help you with the process. Sometimes it helps to have someone else involved because that person can help you better understand each other and come to an agreement together. The mediator might even help you work through the conflict resolution process again to come up with a solution.

Have you ever successfully gone through the conflict resolution process so that everyone ends up happy?

_____

_____

_____

Do you think you're good at the conflict resolution process? Why or why not?

_____

_____

_____

Do you think it's even possible for everyone to be happy with the results of the conflict resolution process?

_____

_____

_____

PRACTICE: TRY RESOLVING THESE CONFLICTS

How would you resolve the following conflicts? Make sure you use the conflict resolution process in your head to work things out.

1. *You and your best friend are watching TV together. You want to watch your favorite show, and your friend wants to watch his or her favorite show. How can you work this out?*

2. *Your friend gave you something that belongs to her brother, and now he wants it back. How can you handle this?*

3. *You borrowed your friend's library book, and now you've lost it. What can you do?*

4. *Your sister always goes into your room and borrows your stuff without asking. How can you work this out?*

5. *Your baby sister or brother ruins your homework. How can you deal with this?*

Resolving a conflict is definitely not always an easy thing to do. Sometimes it can be hard to get everyone to work together, but to resolve the conflict, everyone who is involved must be willing to work together and to accept and do exactly what has been agreed to. Your school may have peer mediators—students who have gone through special training so they can help others work through problems that come up between people. You can also get parents, teachers, and even counselors involved to help you learn the skills you need in order to become a responsible, independent, and confident person who knows how to work through conflicts more easily.

POP QUIZ! CONFLICT RESOLUTION PROCESS

HOW WELL DO YOU UNDERSTAND the process of conflict resolution? Answer the following questions to see if you understand what conflict resolution is. Each question will have more than one correct answer!

1. **What is conflict resolution? (Check all that apply.)**

    ___ Throwing a temper tantrum to get what you want?

___ Working together to understand what the conflict is all about?

___ Finding a solution to the conflict?

___ Getting upset about the conflict?

___ Standing your ground and not being willing to work together?

___ Sorting out the conflict so everyone gets what they want?

2. *What should everyone do to understand the conflict? (Check all that apply.)*

___ Each person should say how he or she feels without being interrupted.

___ Try to make your point heard above everyone else's.

___ Be unwilling to see the other person's point of view.

___ Listen to the other person without interrupting.

___ Put the other person down.

3. *How can you work together? (Check all that apply.)*

___ Make "I" statements such as "I feel hurt when ..."

___ Say what you are feeling without blaming others.

___ Shout to get your point across.

___ Make noises (like "uh-huh," "yes," or "no") in the right places, but without interrupting, to show that you are listening while the other person is talking.

___ Identify what the problem is and find a solution.

4. **How can you find a solution to the problem? (Check all that apply.)**

   ___ Work together to brainstorm.

   ___ State what you want without being to attached to getting your way.

   ___ Write out the issues and discuss each one.

   ___ Think of all possible solutions, even silly ones.

   ___ Get a peer mediator involved.

   ___ Ignore the whole problem and hope it will go away.

5. **What should you remember when you are dealing with conflict resolution? (Check all that apply.)**

   ___ Listen, talk, and brainstorm.

   ___ Argue, shout, and be mean.

___ Understand the conflict and see the other person's point of view.

___ Make mean comments and put the other person down.

___ Look for a solution to the problem, work together, and let others have their say.

___ Work to find the best solution for everyone involved in the conflict.

CONFLICT RESOLUTION PROCESS QUIZ ANSWERS

1. Working together to understand what the conflict is all about; Finding a solution to the conflict; Sorting out the conflict so everyone gets what they want.

2. Each person should say how he or she feels without being interrupted; Listen to the other person without interrupting.

3. Make "I" statements such as "I feel hurt when ..."; Say what you are feeling without blaming others; Make listening noises (like "uh-huh," "yes," or "no") in  the right places, but without interrupting, to show you are listening while the other

person is talking; Identify what the problem is and find a solution.

4. Work together to brainstorm; Write out the issues and discuss each one; Think of all possible solutions, even silly ones; Get a peer mediator involved.

5. Listen, talk, and brainstorm; Understand the conflict and see the other person's point of view; Look for a solution to the problem, work together, and let others have their say; Work to find the best solution for everyone involved in the conflict.

PLAYGROUND POLITICS, PART II

ALL KINDS OF CONFLICTS ARISE on the playground, and they often have to do with picking teams to play some kind of game or deciding what game to play in the first place. If choosing between two games is causing a conflict, try flipping a coin and let that decide which game you'll play, then agree that next time you'll switch it up by playing the other game. When it comes to choosing teams, you take a lot of the conflict out of it by just having everyone count off, then saying that all the even numbers will be one team and all the odd numbers will be the other team!

CHAPTER 6: GROW YOUR SELF-CONFIDENCE

WHAT DOES BEING SELF-CONFIDENT MEAN?

SELF-CONFIDENCE, ALSO KNOWN AS SELF-PRIDE or self-esteem, means feeling proud of yourself. When you have high self-confidence, you feel good about yourself and the things you do, and you also accept that you can't be good at everything. If you have low self-confidence, you don't feel as though you're good at anything, and you blame that on other people.

Being *confident* is not the same as being *cocky*! You know what cocky people are like—they think they're the best at everything and are more than happy to tell you just how good they are at things. That can often leave other people feeling pretty low. Being confident doesn't make other people feel bad.

 High self-confidence is like a shield against all kinds of problems. When you know what your strengths and weaknesses are, you can feel good about yourself, and you'll have a much easier time handling life's rough spots and resisting negative peer pressure. You'll be able to smile and laugh more and just enjoy your life. You are also more realistic and optimistic when you have high self-confidence. Of course, having high self-confidence doesn't mean that you are stuck up or that you think you're better than others—it simply means that you know you are valuable and deserve respect as a person.

Let's find out who you are before we talk about your self-confidence. Write a poem about yourself by filling in the following information. When you're done, read it out loud and see how it sounds. Don't worry about trying to make it rhyme. Remember that not all poetry rhymes! Fill it in however you want.

My name:

_____

Four adjectives that describe me:

_____

I love:

_____

I feel:

_____

I am happy when:

_____

I need:

_____

I give:

_____

I fear:

_____

I would like to see:

_____

I enjoy:

_____

I like to:

_____

I live:

_____

I would like to:

_____

See? You're a poet and didn't even know it! Or maybe you did know it already!

What did you learn about yourself?

_____

_____

Did you learn how you feel about yourself?

_____

BUT WHAT DOES IT LOOK LIKE?

WHEN YOU HAVE HIGH SELF-CONFIDENCE, it doesn't mean that you think you are better than everyone else— it simply means that you feel good about yourself. You can know you have high self-confidence if:

1. You are happy and feel okay as a person.

2. You believe in yourself and look forward to a good future.

3. You enjoy the world around you.

4. You are encouraging to others and respect their differences and your own.

5. You look for ways to be successful, and you look forward to a wonderful future.

Can you think of other things that show you have high self-confidence?

_____

_____

So what do you think? Do you have high self-confidence? Why or why not? Use the space below to jot down your thoughts.

_____

_____

_____

_____

_____

_____

WHAT DOES LOW SELF-CONFIDENCE LOOK LIKE?

WHAT IF YOU REALLY DON'T feel so great about yourself? What does that look like? Here are some things that show what low self-confidence looks like:

1. You feel unhappy and as though you're not as good as everyone else.

2. You have no confidence in yourself and have no hope for your future.

3. You feel miserable or like a victim.

4. You only see the bad things in life and the worst side of everything.

5. You put yourself down, even when someone is saying something nice about you.

Can you think of other things that show low self-confidence?

_____

_____

_____

_____

_____

So what do you think? Do you have low self-confidence? Use the space below to jot down your thoughts.

_____

_____

_____

_____

_____

HOW TO GROW YOUR SELF-CONFIDENCE

IF YOU DO STRUGGLE WITH low self-confidence, you can do something about it! You can build up your self-confidence and begin feeling better about yourself and what you do. Here are some things to try:

1. You can spend time with people who build you up.

2. You can set small, short-term goals that you can reach and then be really happy about. This sets you up to take on bigger goals more successfully!

3. You can learn and practice new things to feel more confident in your abilities.

4. You can be happy and satisfied with who and what you are. After all, you can't be everything to everyone.

5. You can be responsible for yourself and your own actions.

6. Always remember that it's not about being perfect—it's just about making progress in the right direction!

EVEN MORE WAYS TO GROW YOUR CONFIDENCE

YOU CAN MAKE A DIFFERENCE in the way you feel about yourself by aiming for high self-confidence. Everyone has thoughts running through their heads all the time. Some of those thoughts are positive, and some of them are negative. Take a few minutes to think about how you feel about yourself.

You can get a tape recorder and say your thoughts about yourself into it so you can play it back. Now get a piece of paper and draw two boxes. Label one of the boxes positive and one of them negative. As you listen to your recording, put a check in the positive box for every positive statement you hear. For every negative thought, put a check in the negative box. For every negative statement, take the time to think of at least one positive one.

ARE YOU ASSERTIVE, AGGRESSIVE, OR PASSIVE?

ALMOST EVERYONE TENDS TO BE one of three ways: assertive, aggressive, or passive. Which one do you think you are?

Assertive people are able to speak up for themselves in honest and respectful ways. Assertiveness isn't about getting what you need or want by being mean or uncaring. Being assertive means you:

1. Can give your opinions or say how you feel about something respectfully, without being mean.

2. Can ask for what you need or want without hurting someone else.

3. Can give your suggestions and ideas without putting down someone else's suggestions or ideas.

4. Can say no to something you disagree with and not feel bad about it.

5. Can stand up for someone else.

Do you think you are an assertive person? Have you ever done any of the things that an assertive person does?

Aggressive people are forceful and attacking, with or without any reasons for it. When you are aggressive, you attack your friends just because you get mad at them, whether or not there's a reason. You can give your thoughts and opinions without being an aggressive person by learning to control yourself better. You can be the boss of your anger. How can you learn to be the boss of your anger? I'm glad you asked!

You can learn to be in control of your anger by taking the following steps:

1. Take a deep breath in and then breathe out hard.

2. Count to ten before saying anything. If you still feel angry, count to ten again.

3. Walk away from a situation before you say or do something you'll feel bad about later.

4. Use *words* to tell how you're feeling. Don't hurt anyone physically and don't say something mean that you'll feel bad about later on.

5. Say how you feel without raising your voice.

Do you let your anger be the boss of you, or are you the boss of your anger? Use the space below to jot down your thoughts.

_____

_____

Passive people let others use them like a doormat, walk all over them, and mistreat them. They never stand up for themselves or their own wants and  needs. Passive people tend to do the following:

1. Never stand up for their own wants and needs.

2. Never stand up for anyone else.

3. Never disagree with anyone about anything, no matter what, because they try to please everyone.

4. Let other people tell them how to feel or what to think.

5. Don't like sharing their own opinions and ideas, no matter how valuable they are.

Are you a passive person? Do you let everyone else have their own way and treat you badly? Use the space below to jot down your thoughts.

_____

_____

_____

Stand up for yourself! Let people know that it's not okay to be mean to you or put you down. But you also shouldn't be aggressive or mean to them just to make your own point.

When you choose to be more assertive, you're creating a special state of mind. Choosing to be more assertive will send your life in a more positive direction. You'll become much more confident in your ability to get exactly what you want, and you'll be much less likely to be the target of bullying or aggression.

You will also begin seeing your mistakes as ways to improve yourself and learn how to be more in control of your own life instead of letting other people boss you around. Of course, you still have to listen to adults and do what they say (I know, that can be hard sometimes), as long as it's nothing that will hurt you or someone else.

WHEN TALKING TO YOURSELF IS GOOD

AT SOME POINT, SOMEONE WILL probably pick on you and try to hurt your self-confidence. He or she may leave you out of a group or may actually use words to hurt you. Maybe you have a learning disability or have some problems in your family at home. There will *always* be someone around who wants to hurt your self-confidence. You don't have to let that happen! You can use *positive self-talk* to get through those kinds of situations. This is one time when talking to yourself is a good thing! But you might not want to wander around talking *out loud* to yourself, because that might seem a little bit weird to some people. I remember one student who would often mutter out loud to himself, "I'm funny, and people like that about me." Well, people did think he was *funny*, but probably not the way he meant it!

HOW TO DO YOUR OWN POSITIVE SELF-TALK

1. ***Find what are called "trigger words."*** This is a positive phrase that you have a personal connection with that you can repeat whenever you need to in order to make yourself feel better. These words will make you feel more powerful and feel as though you can do anything. Even grown-ups sometimes have "trigger words" that they use to help themselves feel better about things.

2. ***Learn to be comfortable with discomfort.*** I know that sounds weird, but let me explain. There will be times in your life when you will be out of your "comfort zone." You will find yourself in new and unfamiliar situations that might give you a case of the *butterflies*—that kind of nervous, slightly sick feeling when things are really strange. It's okay! This is how you learn about and

experience new things. You can feel those feelings, then let them fade away and do what you need or want to do.

3. **Replace negative things and people in your life with positive ones that will lift you up.** If your friends are negative and never have anything nice to say, it's time to get some new friends. Find friends who will focus on the positive, at least most of the time. It's hard for anyone to be positive *all* the time, but if you can focus on the positive *more* than the negative, you will be on your way to higher self-confidence.

4. **If there is something you are afraid of, put yourself in that situation on purpose (as long as it isn't dangerous).** This will help you see that you really can do anything when you put your mind to it. Fear will hold you back and keep you from achieving your dreams. Break down your fears and spin them into positive action. You will probably find out that it's not nearly as bad as you thought it would be.

5. **Life is full of ups and downs, but you can choose to spend more time focused on the ups than the downs.** When you do that, you will have much higher self-confidence and feel better about your life. This will also help you learn from your

mistakes. When your mind strays toward the negative, focus on the good things you do have in your life rather than the things you don't have.

Having high self-confidence is not about telling yourself or others how much better you are or making yourself look good by making others look bad.

SPEAK KINDLY TO YOURSELF

I am AWESOME

YOU SHOULD ALSO AVOID HAVING low self-confidence that involves telling yourself that you are no good or putting yourself down. Make a habit of speaking kindly to yourself. After all, you're a great kid, right? There is no reason for you to go around beating yourself up by telling yourself you're no good at this or that, or yelling at yourself for making a mistake. *NEVER* tell yourself that you're stupid or dumb! No one is good at everything, and it's not possible to know everything, so don't treat yourself as if you should!

Everyone has times when they feel bad about themselves for whatever reason, but you can avoid giving in to that. When you start having those negative thoughts, switch to more positive thinking. Learn from your mistakes and be happy about all the wonderful things that are going on in your life. If you build up your confidence, you will be happier with yourself and more fun to be around, have lots of friends, and learn to care for yourself and others.

When I was a fifth-grade teacher, I remember one boy in particular who, every time we started trying something new, would always say, "I already know this" or "I'm the best at doing that." It kind of made everyone feel a little bad that they didn't know it or weren't already good at it. He was being *cocky*, not *confident*. Confidence never makes other people feel bad.

CHAPTER 7: FINDING FANTASTIC FRIENDS

WHAT'S SO GREAT ABOUT BEING POPULAR?

POPULARITY IS A VERY COMPLICATED thing. At some point in their lives, almost everyone wishes they could be popular, and some people manage to get there. However, before you risk everything to become popular, there are a few things you should know.

As humans, we are actually hard-wired to be social. It's perfectly natural to want to have friends! For this reason, popularity definitely has its perks. It feels *great* when everyone knows you, wants to be like you, and wants to be friends with you. But it is also important to know the difference between *real* friendships and *superficial* or *fake* friendships.

 When friendships are healthy, they help us live our lives in much happier ways. It is never healthy to always be by yourself. Being popular, however, doesn't always mean that you have *genuine* friendships. Sure, when you're popular, it looks as though you have lots of friends and are always busy. But what happens if popularity is based on superficial things or if it doesn't last? Many tweens are obsessed with how popular they are. Then, when the popularity disappears, they feel ruined. It is important to realize that popularity never lasts, especially if the friendships are mostly fake. While it can be fun and rewarding at times, it should not be confused with *real* friendships.

This doesn't mean you're not allowed to be popular. It simply means that you should put your energy into creating long-lasting, really solid friendships. Some tweens experience a great deal of sadness if they aren't popular or if they are excluded from the popular group. The harder you try to be popular, the less happy you will be.

Remember, when someone becomes popular, it often comes at the expense of a less popular student. When there are popular students, they always outshine the outcasts or the less popular students, and this is not healthy for a good school environment. Some students are rejected and strongly disliked. It is much better to cultivate an atmosphere of acceptance than it is to exclude others.

The most important thing you can do is be friends with people who *genuinely* like you, your personality, and your talents. That way, even when you mess up, you will still have *real* friends to turn to. Liking *yourself* is way more important than being popular.

But, how can you tell if someone is a *real* friend? All friends have their not-so-great moments, but most of the time your friends should encourage you, say positive things about you, and lift you up, not bring you down. If you feel happy around your friends, chances are good that they are having the right kind of influence in your life. If you find that a particular friend insults you, tells you to do bad things, humiliates you, or deserts you, you should reevaluate your friendship with that person!

BEING MORE ASSERTIVE WITH YOUR FRIENDS

FRIENDSHIP IS NOT ALWAYS HUNKY-DORY. Like most people, you may find yourself having a disagreement with your friends. When that happens, you need to be assertive. Let's review what it means to be assertive.

Being assertive is *not* the same as being aggressive or yelling. Being assertive means calmly and respectfully making your opinion clear on an issue. It is important to be assertive when you feel that someone is treating you badly. There is a specific way to go about this to keep from making the situation any worse.

If you feel the need to say you disagree with something, always word it using "I" statements. Never use the word "you," because the other person will feel as though he or she is being blamed. Suppose someone gossiped about you, and you decided to take an assertive approach with that person. Here is how that might go:

"I feel hurt that I was gossiped about."

Or...

"I don't like it that rumors were spread about me."

What do you notice about each of those statements? Neither of them directly accuses the other person in an aggressive way. After all, the whole thing could be a misunderstanding, right? An aggressive statement would be more like the following:

"How dare you talk about me? Who do you think you are?"

As you can see, there is a BIG difference between being aggressive and being assertive. What if it turns out the other person didn't even say the mean thing you thought they said? Being assertive helps solve problems because it means you can express your feelings without directly accusing anyone.

When should you be more assertive? Here are some examples:

- Your friend spreads a rumor or lie about you.

- Someone makes fun of you.

- Someone betrays you.

- Someone tries to get you to do something bad.

Those are just a few examples of times when assertive behavior should be used.

ARE YOUR FRIENDSHIPS HEALTHY OR UNHEALTHY?

HERE ARE SOME SIGNS OF *healthy* friendships:

- They make you feel more alive and cared for. When you hang around someone who is good for you, it should leave you feeling refreshed and full of energy. This is because good friendships create positive, happy energy.

- Healthy friendships allow you to feel whatever you feel. A friend should never pick and choose what you are allowed to feel or express.

- Healthy friendships do not try to prevent you from making friends with other people. A healthy friendship has room for making new friendships with others.

- Healthy friendships accept when the other person changes. Everyone goes through changes. As you grow up, you will begin to see changes in your body such as your height, skin, behavior, moods, voice, and so on. A *real* friend sees past those changes. Healthy friendships do not dissolve just because people go through changes, whether they're good or bad changes.

- Healthy friends are based on *respect*. Not only is it important that you respect the other person, but you should also feel respected by the other person. Respect means you value a person's views and opinions.

- *Both* people benefit from healthy friendships. One person shouldn't be benefiting more than the other person in the friendship. If one person is always asking for favors from the other person, the other person could feel used or hurt. No one should be taken advantage of in a friendship.

- Healthy friendships accept you for exactly who you are. If you are popular, for instance, or part of a clique, it probably means you're trying to be something you are not. You'll be expected to dress, talk, act, and look a certain way in order to fit in. A *real* friend won't require that you change yourself in order to fit in with others. A real friend likes you the way you are.

Here are some signs of unhealthy friendships that you should pay attention to:

- An unhealthy friendship is *possessive*. This means that you are not allowed to have other friends. No one should be controlled in a friendship. You should have the freedom to make friends with anyone you want.

- An unhealthy friendship will try to control your emotions.

- Unhealthy friendships make you feel drained or out of energy.

- Unhealthy friendships try to make you into someone you're not.

- In an unhealthy friendship, there is no loyalty or commitment to each another.

- If you are in an unhealthy friendship, you may be faced with humiliation, gossip, or insults.

THE FRIENDSHIP TRIANGLE

AT SOME POINT IN YOUR life, you may be faced with what is called a *friendship triangle*. A friendship triangle occurs when two of your friends are having a disagreement and you get caught in the middle of it. This type of situation can be difficult because it puts you in a yucky position. Being in a friendship triangle is hard because you will feel pulled in two different directions at the same time. You will feel pressured to go along with one or both friends. This also means that you risk losing your friendship with one or both of your friends, which feels just awful. Whatever you do, don't try to be the mediator! It is not your job to solve the situation. If two of your friends are fighting, they have to figure it out themselves. Let them each know separately that you are not taking sides and that they should fix the problem. If you play mediator, one or both of your friends may end up getting really mad at you.

When you are the person who is being left out of a friendship triangle, it can be very upsetting. It never feels good when suddenly you're the odd person out. How do you deal with this kind of situation? I say you just stay out of the situation for the time being. Do something to distract yourself from the situation. Find or call another friend, or listen to music. You do not have to let yourself be pulled into their drama. Let things cool off for a while and see if it gets better. If it doesn't, you may want to find some different friends.

In some situations, you may be causing one friend to leave the other out. If you are doing this, you should stop it. You may feel that by leaving out one friend, you are gaining more control over the friendship. But what you are really doing is showing your own insecurity. It is important that you change your actions because at some point you may be in the same situation yourself, being the odd person out.

POP QUIZ! TRUE OR FALSE...

1. If you are stuck in the middle of a fight between two friends, you should mediate the situation and relay messages to and from each friend.

2. If you exclude another friend to gain more control over your friendships, you are just showing insecurity.

3. If you feel left out of a friendship triangle, you should to try harder to please the people who are leaving you out.

4. Popularity is far more important than real friendships.

5. If your friend suddenly starts dressing differently, you should still be his or her friend.

6. Even genuine friendships have occasional problems.

7. Good friends make you feel good about yourself.

8. Assertive behavior means standing up for yourself in a calm way.

POP QUIZ!

Use the space underneath each question to jot down your thoughts.

1. Suppose a classmate was rude to you on several occasions. How would you address this situation using assertive behavior?

_____

_____

_____

2. Say what is wrong with the following statement and change it into an assertive statement: "I think you're a very bad person, and I hate the way you treat me."

_____

_____

_____

3. Why are genuine friendships more important than popularity?

_____

_____

_____

_____

CHAPTER 8: YOUR PATHWAY TO EMPOWERMENT

PAVING THE PATHWAY TO EMPOWERMENT

JUST ABOUT EVERYBODY WANTS TO be successful in life, and I'm guessing you're no different in that way. In this chapter, I'm going to give you my absolute BEST EVER advice on how to be an all-around successful person.

I remember one time when I was on a long road trip with my kids, and we got to a long section of the highway where they had torn up all the pavement and it was just dirt. It was really BUMPY, and it made that part of the trip seem much longer. After a few miles of this, we were all feeling pretty uncomfortable. My kids just couldn't understand why there was no pavement. I kept trying to explain to them that they were fixing the road and would pave it soon, but not soon enough for us! This chapter is about helping you pave your own road ahead so it can be as smooth as possible.

GETTING YOUR PRIORITIES RIGHT

YOU'RE A KID, AND YOU should enjoy your childhood while you can! The older you get, the more responsibilities you will have. You may already notice this happening. Perhaps you're on a sports team, or you're participating in a new extracurricular activity that takes a lot of your time and energy. Meanwhile, you're also expected to do your homework, study for tests and quizzes, and still have time to spend with your friends and family. You may be asking yourself how in the world you can possibly set priorities when you're distracted by so many different things. Believe it or not, it's possible to have time for everything that's important in your daily life, including your friends, family, schoolwork, and after-school activities.

If you take the following steps, you will be able to set the right priorities and make time for everything that is important in your life.

1. **The first step to setting priorities is to understand how you are spending your time.**

If you want to manage your time better, you need to know how you're spending it in the first place! Write down every activity that you do and try to figure how much time you spend doing each one.

Make your list here, then estimate how much time you spend on that activity.

_____

_____

_____

_____

_____

_____

2. *Set up a new priority list for yourself—one that allows you to spend enough time with each of the most important areas in your life.*

If you need to spend more time doing extracurricular activities, indicate that on your priority list. I'm asking you to put your priorities in a new order. To do this, ask yourself the following questions:

What is most important in my life these days?

_____

_____

_____

In which areas of my life do I want to spend more time?

_____

_____

_____

In which areas of my life would I be okay spending a little less of my time?

_____

_____

_____

Where do I waste my time?

_____

_____

_____

SETTING GOALS—THE SMART WAY TO GO!

ONCE YOU HAVE FIGURED OUT what your priorities are, the next step is to set small goals. What exactly is a goal? A goal is something you want to achieve, something that you work up to. For example, if you wanted to get on the baseball team, that would be a goal. In order to achieve a goal, you need to outline the steps you have to take to reach that goal.

Suppose one of your goals is to score an A on your next math test. Here is an example of the steps you could take in order to reach that goal:

1. Put more time into understanding math homework.

2. Meet with your teacher to discuss math exercises.

3. Practice 20 new math problems each day.

If you take the time to figure out all the small steps that will get you there, you can achieve really big goals! There will be mistakes along the way, to be sure. Everyone experiences some failure along the way to achieving his or her goals. Don't let this discourage you from achieving your dreams. Learn from your mistakes and keep going!

DOES GOAL SETTING REALLY HELP?

Setting goals can really help you a LOT. The first benefit is that you are more likely to achieve your dreams if you set goals. This is because without goals, you'll lack direction and you won't know how to steer yourself in the right direction.

Another benefit of goal setting is that it can increase your confidence and your self-esteem. When you have something to work on each day, it makes you feel very important and confident in yourself.

Finally, goal setting at this age will prepare you for all kinds of things in your future. If you get used to setting goals now, it is a tool that you can use during your entire life. For example, when you're in high school, you will have to set goals around things like applying for college, taking entrance exams, and much more. Once you're in college, you will have to set more goals to finish your courses and graduate with a degree. After this, you'll have a career, and you will have to set goals for that as well. And you may someday want to see all 50 states or learn how to make furniture or a quilt, and you'll have to set a goal for that. I hope you can see that goal setting is something you can use your whole life to do the things you need and want to do. That's why you want to master it now rather than later.

KEEPING YOURSELF MOTIVATED

In order to achieve your goals, you will need to be motivated. It can be hard to stay on track with your goals, especially when there are so many distractions all around you. One way to stay motivated is to remind yourself of what you're trying to do. In other words, *keep your eyes on the prize*! I know that studying for a math or science test may not feel like much fun, but if it's a necessary step in reaching your goals, just think how wonderful you'll feel when you get there!

Another great way to keep up your motivation is to give yourself a prize every time you complete a step toward your goals. For example, you may hold off on a special treat or TV show until you've completed your studies or homework. This will make you want to study so you can get your little prize.

You can also learn to enjoy the steps of getting to your goal and not just the big ending. If you don't, you might slack off. Rewards are a great way to stay motivated, but remember to also find the parts of everything that are fun and enjoy them!

YOU CAN MAKE SMART CHOICES

ON THE PATHWAY TO ACHIEVING your dreams, you have to be in charge of getting yourself there. To reach success, you need to make smart choices. Most of the time, your body will give you what people call a "gut feeling" to signal that something is wrong or right. Here are some smart choices I have found that help kids achieve their dreams:

✓ Always listen and take notes in class, study for exams, and complete homework on time.

✓ Get involved in extracurricular activities or sports.

✓ Have a healthy social and family life.

The choices you make now will set your future. You should always ask yourself the right questions to avoid bad behaviors. For example, suppose you are considering watching a TV show or hanging out with friends the night before a really big test. You'd probably want to do those things rather than study, right? But ask yourself the following questions in those kinds of situations:

1. If I decide to slack off instead of study, how will this hurt me in the future?

2. What will be the end result if I don't study?

3. How will a bad grade affect me?

4. How will a bad grade affect the rest of the school year?

5. How will a bad grade affect my future?

6. If I choose to study instead of slack off, how will I feel afterward?

7. How will studying benefit my grade in this class?

8. How will a good grade positively affect my future?

When you ask these kinds of questions, it helps you realize the long-term effects of your actions. Every action you take, whether big or small, affects your future. If you make smart choices instead of poor ones, you will build a very bright future for yourself. Hard work and smart choices will help you do great in class, in academics, in extracurricular activities, and in your future. Whether you are in elementary school or middle school, everything you do now will affect you further down the line.

HOW TO STAY FOCUSED
WHEN YOU NEED TO

THESE DAYS, KIDS AND TEENS have so many fun distractions all around them. Whether it's your tablet computer, the TV, or your cell phone, there are tons of reasons to lose focus and use one of your hi-tech gadgets. All these devices are great, but you should never let them distract you from your priorities, nor should they stop you from reaching your goals.

One way to stay focused is to just turn off these things while studying unless you actually need them. Shutting down your computer won't help if you use it for your homework. But you probably don't need the Internet, email, or your phone to be on, so shut those off.

Of course, everyone needs to socialize, and it's important to set aside time to talk with your friends. After you complete your homework and studies, set aside a special time to watch TV or talk to friends, as long as this doesn't keep you from your academics or getting enough sleep. Balance is important!

As a kid, a lot of thoughts are probably running through your head every single second. Sometimes all you need to do to get focused is to clear and calm your mind. How do you do that? It's easier than you might think! First, close your eyes and breathe deeply to get relaxed. Then think of a single object in your mind, and keep that object in mind. Then focus all your attention on that single image you are imagining in your mind. Do this until all other thoughts have gone away.

Many people listen to classical music in order to stay focused. If your academic performance needs an extra boost, try listening to Mozart, Beethoven, or any other classical music.

Sometimes doing a whole pile of homework all at once can be hard. Whether or not you have a limited attention span, taking short breaks can really help. Just a quick break to run around a little bit can get your heart pumping and clear your mind. You will find that by taking short breaks, you'll be less likely to run out of steam during your studies.

PERSEVERANCE AND NEVER GIVING UP

No one can succeed without perseverance! If you want to reach your goals, you can't give up. Even if you fail to do one of your steps, you can't stop trying. It's completely normal to have mistakes and setbacks along the way. Did you know that the most successful people in the world have failed more than once before reaching success?

It is important to learn from all your failures and your mistakes in order to achieve your goals.

POP QUIZ!

Describe how to properly set goals.

_____

_____

_____

Name a few examples of smart choices that will help you reach your dreams.

_____

_____

_____

How can you figure out your priorities?

_____

_____

_____

How can you stay on track for reaching goals?

_____

_____

_____

CONCLUSION

CONGRATULATIONS! YOU'VE READ THIS WHOLE book! Do you feel as though you've just finished running a long race? Whew! But it's a good feeling, isn't it? Do you realize that by finishing this book, you just learned about all kinds of things that will help you make a much smoother shift into becoming a *teenager*? Now, that IS exciting!

And that's why I wrote this book for YOU. I've seen far too many tweens have a really tough time during the sensitive years from ages 9 to 12, so I wanted to share with you what I've learned from my years as a mom, a teacher, and a school counselor that can make it easier for YOU.

Now you have a whole book full of really great tips and tools for handling all sorts of things, from bullying and cyberbullying to peer pressure and cliques, from conflict resolution and self-confidence to friendships and success.

You might also be feeling a bit overwhelmed by how much I've shared with you. In fact, you may feel as though your head is stuffed so full that you don't even know where to begin! Trust me, I understand how you're feeling because I felt the exact same way when I sat down to start writing this book! That's why I'm going to list some of the most important things I've shared with you so you can easily remember them.

TAKE CARE OF YOURSELF

✓ Speak kindly to yourself.

✓ Like who you are, even if you want to make some changes for the better.

✓ Being nice makes you happier than being popular.

✓ Grow your self-confidence.

✓ Stand up for yourself. You deserve to be treated fairly and with respect, and you don't have to give in to negative peer pressure.

✓ Figure out your priorities.

✓ Set goals for yourself (start small) and figure out all the steps you need to take to get there.

✓ Never give up!

✓ Learn from your mistakes and failures.

✓ Remember, it's not about being perfect, it's about making progress in the right direction.

TAKE CARE OF OTHERS

✓ Be kind to others. You know now that bullying and cyberbullying can hurt people for the rest of their lives, so don't do it! Help stop it from happening.

✓ Be a *real* friend. You know how great it feels to have *real* friends, so be one yourself!

✓ Never start or join a clique. Cliques leave people out and make them feel awful.

✓ Practice conflict resolution to find solutions that work for everyone when problems come up.

Thanks for reading, and I wish you every success!

AUTHOR ERAINNA WINNETT

ERAINNA WAS BORN AND RAISED in central Louisiana. The oldest of five children she always yearned to be a teacher and forced her siblings to play school year round. Naturally, she graduated with a teaching degree in 1995 and earned her master's degree in 2000. Five years later she earned her education specialist degree in early childhood education. After fifteen years in the classroom, she moved to the role of school counselor and has never been happier.

While serving as school counselor at an elementary school in northeast Texas, she frequently uses children's books as therapy to help her students heal, learn and grow. Ideas for her books come from the students she works with on a daily basis. Her goal, as an author, is to touch the hearts of children, one story at a time. Erainna lives on a 300 acre cattle ranch near the Red River with her husband, two daughters, three dogs, two horses, and one ill-tempered cat.

To see more books by Erainna, please visit her counseling website counselingwithheart.com.

TWEEN SUCCESS SERIES ALSO INCLUDES:

TWEEN TIME:
A TWEEN'S GUIDE to
ACADEMIC SUCCESS

Tweens today have a hard time trying to figure out how to make it all happen in their lives. They are pulled in too many directions and feel like there are too many demands on their time. All of this is happening during the most sensitive and difficult years of their lives: The transition years from pre-teen to teen, which roughly covers ages 9-12. It can leave tweens and their families feeling helpless and hopeless. But there is a better way!

Child education and counseling expert Erainna Winnett brings more than 20 years of experience in teaching, counseling and raising children to the challenges tweens face. Written in a conversational style and filled with real tips and strategies, *Tween Time* will help any tween become more successful in school and at home while still finding time to just be a kid.

Tween Time covers the following topics: Optimal Organization, Finding Time for Fun-Time, Homework Help, Study Tips, and Test Prep.

Made in the USA
Lexington, KY
31 May 2016